the true book of

The MOONWALK ADVENTURE

By Margaret Friskey

CHILDRENS PRESS, CHICAGO

For Jeff, who learned to read
in the year of the first moonwalk

All photographs courtesy of
National Aeronautic and Space Administration
Houston, Texas
Cover: Apollo 12 on the moon

Library of Congress Catalog Card Number: 76-123803

1 2 3 4 5 6 7 8 9 10 11 12 13 14 15 16 17 18 19 20 21 22 23 24 25 R 75 74 73 72 71 70

The MOONWALK ADVENTURE

Apollo 12 Lunar Module in lunar landing configuration with astronauts Charles Conrad, Jr. and Alan L. Bean aboard. Taken by Richard Gordon, Jr., Command Module pilot, who remained with the Command and the Service modules in lunar orbit.

In the year 1969, men walked on the moon.

They came from the planet Earth. They traveled about 240,000 miles through dark outer space beyond the earth to get there.

The first men who walked
on the moon looked out on
a strange world.

There were holes called
craters.

There was no water.

There was no air.

There was no wind.

There was no sound.

There was very little
color.

There were no living things
on the moon.

Taken by Apollo 11 astronauts Neil A. Armstrong, commander, and Edwin E. Aldrin, Jr., Lunar Module pilot. Michael Collins, Command Module pilot, remained with the Command and Service modules in lunar orbit.

One after the other, the first two men to walk on the moon left their ship.

They had to take air with them.

They did not know just what they would step into on the moon.

They could see rock dust.

But they did not know how deep it was.

Astronaut Edwin E. Aldrin, Jr., Apollo 11 Lunar Module pilot, descends steps of Lunar Module ladder as he prepares to walk on the moon. Taken by astronaut Neil A. Armstrong, commander, with a 70 mm lunar surface camera.

The rock dust was not deep.

But the men could see their footprints in it.

The rays of the sun were very hot.

There was no blanket of air around the moon to shelter it from the hot rays.

Nights on the moon were very cold.

The men wore space suits to protect them.

Apollo 11 on the moon. Astronaut Edwin E. Aldrin, Jr. has just deployed the Solar Wind Composition experiment. Taken by Neil A. Armstrong, commander.

The men had a metal marker
to leave on the moon.
It was called a plaque.
They carried it fastened
to the ladder on the landing-
gear strut of the Lunar Module.
Words on the marker said:

HERE MEN FROM THE PLANET EARTH
FIRST SET FOOT UPON THE MOON
July, 1969, A.D.
WE CAME IN PEACE FOR ALL MANKIND

Closeup of the plaque which the Apollo 11 astronauts carried to the moon attached to the ladder on the landing-gear strut on the Lunar Module. It was covered with a thin sheet of stainless steel during flight.

The men found it was easy
to walk and work on the moon.
Things do not weigh much
on the moon. The pull of the
moon, called gravity, is much
less than the gravity on the
earth.

It is this pull of gravity
that gives things weight.

They learned many things.

And they left instruments
that would keep sending more
information to Earth, after
they had left.

Astronaut Edwin E. Aldrin, Jr., Apollo 11 Lunar Module pilot, walking toward a position to set up two components of the Early Apollo Scientific Experiments Package. Taken by Astronaut Neil A. Armstrong, commander.

The men on the moon did not have much time.

The air that they brought with them would be gone in about two hours.

They worked fast to set up the instruments that would be left behind.

Astronaut Edwin E. Aldrin, Jr., Apollo 11 Lunar Module pilot, is deploying the Passive Seismic Experiment Package. The Laser Ranging Retro-Reflector can be seen to the left and farther in the background.

Neil A. Armstrong was the first man to step on the moon.

He took this picture of Edwin E. Aldrin, Jr., who was with him.

You can see the reflection of Neil Armstrong in the helmet of Edwin Aldrin.

Apollo 11 on the moon. Edwin E. Aldrin, Jr. walks on the moon toward Neil A. Armstrong, who took this picture with a 70 mm lunar surface camera.

It was time to get
ready for the long trip
back to Earth.

Astronaut Edwin E. Aldrin, Jr., Apollo 11 Lunar Module pilot, walks on the surface of the moon near the leg of the Lunar Module.

This strange-looking craft
is called a Lunar Module.

Lunar comes from a Latin
word meaning "moon."

Edwin E. Aldrin, Jr., pilot,
and Neil A. Armstrong, commander,
will leave the moon in the top
section of the Lunar Module.

The bottom section, used to
land on the moon, will be left
behind.

Apollo 11 on the moon. Edwin E. Aldrin, Jr. at the equipment bay of the descent stage of the Lunar Module. It was here that scientific equipment for the lunar landing mission was stored during flight.

From inside the Lunar Module, the men took a picture of the flag of the United States on the moon.

Since there is no wind on the moon, the flag is held out by a wire.

Footprints of the first men on the moon can be seen all around the flag.

The flag of the United States, deployed on the surface of the moon, dominates this picture taken from inside the Apollo 11 Lunar Module.

Edwin Aldrin, pilot of the
Lunar Module, took a picture of
Neil Armstrong, commander.

The men were in the Lunar
Module ready for lift-off.

The lift-off was timed so
that the Lunar Module could meet
and dock with the parent ship.

Astronaut Michael Collins,
in the parent ship, had been
orbiting the moon, waiting for
the moonwalkers to return.

Astronaut Neil A. Armstrong, Apollo 11 commander, back inside the Lunar Module while it still rests on the lunar surface.

As the Lunar Module left the moon, the men saw a wonderful earth-rise beyond the moon's horizon.

Apollo 11 Lunar Module ascent stage during rendevous in lunar orbit. Astronaut Michael Collins, who remained in orbit around the moon in the Command and Service modules, took this picture.

The men in the Lunar Module
saw the parent ship.
It would take them back
to Earth.
Now the surface of the moon
was far below them.

The Apollo 11 Command and Service modules are photographed from the Lunar Module in lunar orbit.

Now the moon looked smaller.

It looked like a big ball of rock in the darkness of outer space.

It looked smaller and smaller as the spaceship sped toward Earth.

This photograph of the moon was taken from the Apollo 8 spacecraft in orbit around the moon.

The earth seemed to grow larger.

Blue water of its oceans could be seen.

White clouds drifted in the blanket of air that sheltered the earth.

View of the earth photographed by the Apollo 8 astronauts on their return trip from orbiting the moon. The sun reflection is within the Indian Ocean.

The earth looked like this
from 98,000 miles away.
The whole continent of Africa
could be seen.

Apollo 11 view of Earth. Most of Africa and portions of Europe and Asia can be seen in this spectacular photograph.

From a little over 22,000 miles, the earth looked like this.

The men began to get ready to bring their spaceship through the earth's atmosphere to a safe landing.

The earth from 22,300 miles in space. NASA's Applications Satellite (ATS)-III transmitted this color photo back to a ground station at Rosman, N.C., Nov. 10, 1967. South America is clearly visible.

The first men who walked on the moon returned safely on July 24, 1969.

They were back on the planet Earth.

There was water.

There was air.

There was wind.

There was sound.

There was lots and lots of color.

And there were living things.

The three Apollo 11 astronauts, Neil A. Armstrong, Edwin E. Aldrin, Jr., and Michael Collins, await pickup by helicopter from the U.S.S. *Hornet*. The fourth man in the life raft is a U.S. Navy underwater demolition team swimmer. All men are wearing biological isolation garments.

HIGHLIGHTS OF THE APOLLO PROGRAM

Many unmanned flights in the Apollo Program tested the equipment needed for a flight to the moon.

In October, 1968, Apollo 7 was launched with a three-man crew aboard. Astronaut Walter M. Shirra, Jr., commander, with Donn Eisele and Walter Cunningham, in an eleven-day mission orbiting the earth, made sure that the moonship equipment was ready to make the long trip to the moon and return the men to Earth.

In December, 1968, Apollo 8 with Frank Borman, commander, and James Lovell, Jr. and William Anders, left the earth's orbit and sped to the moon. They orbited the moon ten times, but did not land on it.

In July, 1969, the flight of Apollo 11 carried three men to the moon. Michael Collins, Command Module pilot, remained with the Command and Service modules in lunar orbit while Neil A. Armstrong, commander, and Edwin E. Aldrin, Jr., Lunar Module pilot, landed on the moon and walked upon it— a historic moment seen around the world through the miracle of live television.

In November, 1969, the Apollo 12 Lunar Module landed on the moon with astronauts Charles Conrad, Jr., commander, and Alan L. Bean, Lunar Module pilot. Astronaut Richard F. Gordon, Jr. remained in the Command and Service modules in lunar orbit.

In April, 1970, Apollo 13 with Captain James Lovell, Fred Haise, and John Swigert, was 200,000 miles on its way toward the moon when an explosion blew out the side of the Service Module. In spite of this, they circled the moon and returned safely to Earth with the help of the Lunar Module and the ground crew.

The Apollo Program has opened the way for further explorations of the moon, and even of some of the planets in our solar system.

For every astronaut on a spaceflight mission there are thousands of people on Earth who make the trip possible. Moon flights are an almost unbelievable technical achievement. Thousands of dedicated people have worked toward this end.

It is a Saturn rocket
that provides the
thrust that sends
a spacecraft
to the moon.

The first stage
of the rocket
fires and lifts
the heavy load.
It falls away
about 2½ minutes
after lift-off.

The second stage fires,
sending the spacecraft
into orbit about 100
miles above the earth
at a speed of
about 18,000 miles
an hour. Then
it falls away.

The third stage
is fired once
to put the space-
craft in the right
orbit around the
earth. At just
the right moment
it is fired again.
This gives the
spacecraft a
speed of more than
24,000 miles an
hour. This speed
is needed to break
away entirely
from the earth's
pull of gravity.

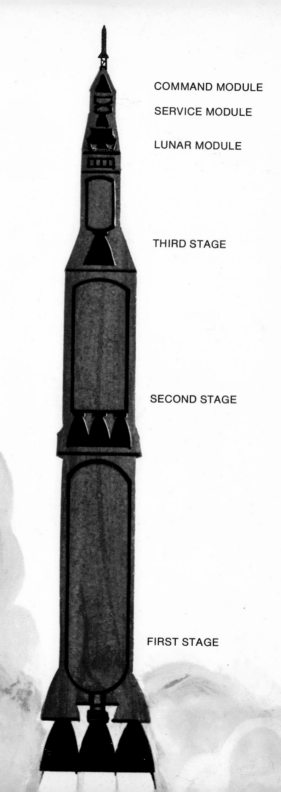

COMMAND MODULE

SERVICE MODULE

LUNAR MODULE

THIRD STAGE

SECOND STAGE

FIRST STAGE

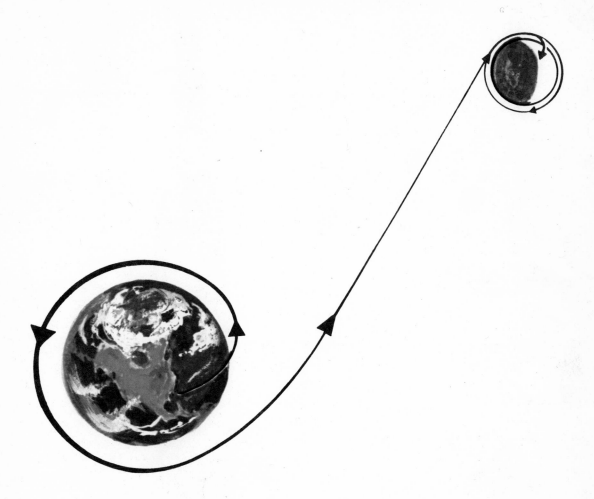

The moon is not standing still. It is traveling in an orbit around the earth. Also, the earth is turning on its axis and speeding around the sun, taking its moon with it.

This is why the spacecraft orbits the earth until it can head for the moon at just the right moment. Then, breaking away completely from the earth's pull of gravity, the weightless craft streaks toward its target—moon—almost a quarter of a million miles away.

At right. Apollo training. Astronaut Michael Collins participates in training exercise in the Apollo Mission Simulator in Building 5.